Spiritual Reflections

Through Meditation and Reflection

Written as spiritually inspired writings
Given as Spiritual Talks at Sunday Service's

Written by
Doris Nickles

AuthorHouse™
1663 Liberty Drive
Bloomington, IN 47403
www.authorhouse.com
Phone: 1-800-839-8640

© 2010 Doris Nickles. All rights reserved.

No part of this book may be reproduced, stored in a retrieval system, or transmitted by any means without the written permission of the author.

First published by AuthorHouse 2/16/2010

ISBN: 978-1-4490-7924-6 (e)
ISBN: 978-1-4490-7922-2 (sc)
ISBN: 978-1-4490-7923-9 (hc)

Library of Congress Control Number: 2010900966

Printed in the United States of America
Bloomington, Indiana

This book is printed on acid-free paper.

Table of Contents

Writer's Introduction 1

Today's Choices 3

The Gift 6

What If I Knew 14

Power Powerless 19

A Part of the Circle of Life 21

Continued Pursuit of Healing 27

My Walk My Talk with God 32

Reading from the Greber Bible 39

Live My Own Life 43

A Soul's Life 48

Holistic Fitness 52

You Are Not Walking Alone 59

The Green Not of a Spiritualists Life 62

Law of Love 67

Law of Love Part Two 74

God's Loving Laws to Live By 78

Writer's Introduction

High my name is Doris; I've always loved to write for as long as I can remember. I write about many things, but, it all relates back to the life I have experienced. My first published writing piece was in High School, a short essay report on basketball, and song interpretation. I say I love to write because I do, but, if my language arts teacher had anything to say about it, it would be that I struggled with the lessons and applying them correctly in my writing.

I decided to publish my writings in 2002, out of encouragement from friends and church members. Most of what I had written in my first book came from writing for therapy, when I hit a difficult point in my life. My world was crashing around me. Personal crisis, family crisis, and career crisis all happening at the same time. I started to journal and some how, it transitioned into poetry, sonnets, and short essays. I was praying through my writing, and disclosing through my writing, my pain, sadness, and as well my gratitude in life, and my happiest moments. I took a chance and put it in print, for the world to read. Many read my book, and found they could relate in many ways to what I shared.

My first book was a local success, and was very satisfying to me. In it I also shared photo's that were taken at the time of each piece I wrote, they were sights that inspired me. I just had to include them, making it a unique book to read and keep. That book was "Lighting the Heart a Healing of the Soul"

I hope in sharing these short essays it is welcomed by many, and in reading them one can appreciate how I share the inspirations I receive from my many spirit friends. Most of the inspirations come from meditations, some done when trying to find answers, others done for understanding life's lessons. There are those writings as well that help to heal the inner being, struggling to get through difficult times. I could write a very large book on my life experiences and adventures, but, I would never finish and publishers would have difficulties putting the book together. So I decided I would write in small parcels, and just put a smaller book out with what I am told are my best and welcomed writings, known as talks that I have given in church.

Oh yes, I should mention I have shared these writings in the church I belong to, "The Spiritualist Church of Devine Guidance". I am a certified Medium and Healer. I am an accomplished Nurse, Mother of three, a certified Councilor, and a soon to be ordained Minister.

In my life I have survived two major motor vehicle accidents, a divorce, alcoholism and addictions, one child almost died from Leukemia, another almost died in a motor vehicle accident, and was left brain injured, but remains a wonderful person. My family has survived many ups and downs, a separate book I could write, and many would find hard to believe, but my family and friends know all about it. As you read the writings keep an open mind to the things that are happening in your own life, and you may start hearing the special vibrations of spirit, inspiring you to find strength and answers that you need. Welcome to my writings and I hope they are enjoyable. Thank you for allowing me to share with you.

Sincerely Doris

Today's Choices

Today I have a choice, to do my best that is all that is required. "My Best", take care of self, meditate daily, think things out, talk with my guides, and my higher power, walk through my day, as an offer to God, to do his will, not, mine. Here today, I must have personal responsibility, loving myself, as I love others.

All I do creates all I reap. All I am, as when growing a garden, the work that is done, produces, what I harvest.

Today I will try to live through these 24 hours only. I will not try to tackle my whole life's problems, all at once. For today I might have to deal with something upsetting, or that, might appall me, if I had to do it for a lifetime. I will deal with it positively for today.

Today I can be happy- it is just the beginning. I will arm myself with positives, I will walk my day knowing, I have a higher power, on my side, and spirit guides all around me. I can be as happy, as I choose to be, it is all a matter of where, I set my mind to be at.

Today I will make adjustments to myself, to accommodate for what comes along, to challenge me. Instead of trying to adjust everything to my own desires. I will accept my luck (as some call it), as it comes in my path. I am able to fit myself to it. God isn't asking me to change the world, only to change me, if needed in my world.

Today I want to strengthen my mind; I have an interest in life, and living it to my best. I have a choice if I want to grow. So I study, I learn something useful: The key word is "useful".

I have a choice to not loaf around mentally or, physically.

What I choose to learn, is my choice, but, it should require effort, thought, and concentration. A challenge I can meet.

Today I will not only take on a mental challenge, but, I will challenge my soul. I will do this by doing a good turn, without thought of credit, or being discovered. If this happens it will not count. Further more, I might consider doing a few things; I don't want to do, just for the exercise. Something like asking for good things to happen for someone I may not like, or has hurt me. Lending a helping hand, in a task someone else has, even if I don't like it, and don't have to.

I also will not show hurt of feelings, even if they are hurt. Just for today, keeping a positive flow of thought and energy.

Today I can choose to be more agreeable, look as good as I can, dress nicely, talk softly, and be courteous and polite. I will have patience, even if time is tight. I will reserve my critical statements, even if I feel deserving to say it. I will refrain from finding fault, and not try to improve anything, or any body, but myself.

For today, I have a program, I may not always follow it exactly, but, I have one, and I have a choice in following it, but I am also human. I will however spare myself, as best as possible, from hurry, and indecision.

I will give myself a quiet half hour, to relax, and recharge. I will look for a positive perspective within my life, in which to grow on.

I will choose not to be afraid. Never fearing my enjoyment of what is beautiful in life. I am as others are, entitled to good living and loving, of what is good in life.

My smile is mine, no one should I let take it away. I believe

I give a simple smile and sometimes a simple hug, back to the world, and the world will give one back to me.

Personal responsibility means, I get in my garden of life, what I plant, care for, and nurture, all I put in, is all that I may receive back. I hope for today, my choice taken, has done for others, what I want and receive for me. Just for today. Thank you to God, My Spirit Guides, and a spiritual program, that guides me through a better life seen.

The Gift

Upon this holiday season, joy, and hope to
Build, our Hearts filled and gay
Excitement and wonderment heighten
Toward the big day
It is a season I wish could last the whole
Year through
Happy and gay not just for the carols, gifts,
And parties too
But for the love all portray

This season is a time, where most of us
Release
Love, understanding, and tolerance
Not just with loved ones, but others as well,
Our paths meet by chance
A visible kindness from our hearts and mind
Flow Free to all, no hesitance
Where God's love, light, and energy, reside
Within our hearts with radiance

Why is it, this hidden gift only revealed at
Special times or events
Loves sweetness, meant to be seen by all
And to all around us
We seem to think; more should show,
The arrival, of a jolly soul, to us
I believe, this time to remind us, is meant to
Be year round for all of us

This holiday season, what comes to
Mind
Magical times and sugar plums
Especially when hearing words of cheer,
And gifts to come
Secrets of joy, in finding that special gift,
For that special someone

From our hearts, to our minds
We hear poetry and tales of the poor giving
Their all
Giving a gift, with all their love, no
Hesitation at all
Given with love, and sincerity, no regrets
At all
No monetary value remains as the last
Is given, for the love of all

We all have gifts with a greater value
A price cannot be placed on these so true
As much as I would like to be Santa all the
Year through
I can be a part of the light of God, in my life
Honest and true

God gave us the gift of knowledge and free
Will,
Love, kindness and caring
Some of us have even more to offer
With no sparing
If we polish and develop these for the
Highest and best mastering
A value improved through interest in these
Gifts of offering

Through mind, body, and soul, we find the
Gift of healing
Able to communicate, between spirit world
And living world
Message delivering to all needing
This gift from spirit world, teaching,
Guiding and Directing

All we need do, with love and devotion,
Sincere and pure,
To spirit we are offering
We were given hearts that feel
Souls that connect the mind all guidance
Revealed
The creative part of us, drawn on, and
Demonstrated

With a pleasant appeal
Our brain, we all know is calculative and
Literal
Processes and files many important details
That accumulate
To interact intellectually, and create great
Debates
Also given physical strength in order to
Survive, and populate

Important in life to survive, is also a
Spiritual side to locate
Helping and guiding us to be good, and do
Right and abide
Sort through the not so good, and repair our
Harmony,
Flowing with the tide

This should be all year through, not just in a
Season
Of good will and glad tidings
Through past lessons and times of growth in
Life with standing
I have learned to give of self to those around
In need or strife

I have accepted, wealth or not, I will survive
In this my life
For my wealth is not measured in amount of
Coin,
But in all the good I do in life
God in his wisdom created our universe,

Universal energy flowing all around
Our human being containing self will and
Self reliance found
So many talents to discover, a life to live
Today, I too am bound
Rich in love, deep sincere caring, energy
From within heart and soul found
My creativity with words, and listening
Skills abound

These I am polishing even as I write these
Words, I feel in me
I bake many good things, the secret
Ingredient; love within me a free will
Many things I do for others,
Bring a smile, and joy for I fulfilled
Again all given freely and full of love,
A secret to me and no one else

Many talents, I could list, or still discover,
A journey of love
As it is used, as needed, for each deed I do,
Comes, from God's plan above
No ego here, only self inventory, what I can
Offer up to God, and Spirits love
Gifts born within me, received from
My creator above

Spirits help to polish and develop,
One day at a time, no fear
No matter my many trials and troubles in
Life to Occur
With spirit help and strength, I shine through
Innocence and hope, faith and belief,
All built with trust so sure

A belief growing through the years, with
Unconditional love a must
Tolerance, sensitivity, acceptance learned,
A heart guided by spiritual trust
These gifts applied to enhance me,
As an instrument, I am focused
Making way for spirit work and healing
A must

A privilege and honor to be useful, oh what
A Feeling
A very big world in need of healing
My small part of this world, I am given
A chance in healing
A gift discovered through guidance,
And lessons,
Brought by spirit being to communicate
Through me, to others, I offer to Spirit

A communication that breaks through
Barriers, to those who seek it
A guiding energy of love indeed, to you,
To me,
From spirit direct be it for love, healing,
Or guidance in effect
Strengthens to build goodness in our world

Perception, enhancing and improving,
A healing ability, spirit offers my world
Forever grateful for this developed ability
Spirit enters my world
God's greatest gift, of energy, and
Love
Christ's White light fills our world

Given by God our father, are the gifts I
Speak of,
His Plans are clear in this season, it is
Heightened and visible, meant to be
Demonstrated through the year
May we all recognize our gifts without
Doubt or fear
A chance we have to share with others,
Our gifts with cheer

Accept what has been received given freely
The known gift
Return from the heart, with sincere thought,
From you a gift
Peace and harmony filling us always,
Another great gift
God's love and blessings the greatest gift

Understanding, all powerful gifts,
Within a heart so real
Together in thought for spirituality of the
Individual
May we realize we are the answer to mans appeal
Love, peace, and harmony God blesses all of us.

What If I Knew

There was a day where my mind was clear, and my thoughts were free, and UN prejudice. I believe I was driving to work that morning when my first thought came to me, at an infamous corner street, I drive by all the time. There were some people streaming out of one of the corner buildings. They were definitely, overcome with reminders of the night before, in the form of hangovers, bad adventures while intoxicated, and a look of lost souls within them.

I thought, "I wonder what their lives were like prior to the point in life they were at." It hit me, "what if I knew!" Would it make a difference in my attitude towards them? (Not that I have a bad attitude, as I care for people daily from all walks of life). I don't always know what brings them to the point in life they are at, when I meet them. I know how I was raised, protected, discipline, loved, cared for, provided for, but, not spoiled in the sense, of not knowing the value of what is in life.

I didn't come from a life of unlimited privileges, or freedom. There were appropriate limits, rules, morals, and ethics in the lives of my family.

So what is it that happens for those I see in despair, destitution, troubles in the present or even pain from various ailments? Was their life harsh, were they loved and cared for the way that was needed? Was this something they chose to end up in, through their free will, and predetermined personality? By this I mean the addictive personality, or the weakened psychic, not under their obvious control, or understanding.

There were so many thoughts as to what history was behind the troubled being.

That's where the thought of "What if I knew," came into my mind.

I am working toward my Mediumship. One that provides healing, guidance, and assistance in troubled times for others. I wonder if it is important, to feel and understand what is there, in their auras of the past, and present. As a medium, I do readings from time to time, for those requesting assistance, I feel privileged, that I can help others this way. But sometimes, or rather most times, I may never have met these people before their reading; yet, they all seem to say the same thing at the end of the reading, "You really hit it dead on," "like you knew me." Meanwhile I don't.

I am glad sometimes though, that I don't know ahead of time. I am also a sympathetic person, very emotional, and I feel for others, and their pain. I think I would be ill, if I knew too much. Thank God I really do not remember anything of the readings I give.

So what if I knew then when I work with others daily, assessing and helping them. It doesn't really matter if I know anything ahead of time. I realize it is the feelings, sensing, and hearing, of what is behind that person's need, that is important.

I don't need to know if they were abused in a certain way, or they have an addiction of a specific type, or they have done terrible sins, in a specific detail. All I need to know is they are troubled or in need, or that they are ok, just searching for something more in their life. That is where the sensing is really important, and that seeing, and hearing what is there is an extra tool in helping and guiding another person.

I could have a really cushy well paying job, 9 – 5, Monday to Friday, but I may not be happy with it, if I am not feeling satisfied that, I am helping others. I think at times, that is my addiction in life at the moment. I always want to help; I always want to fix things, in a humanistic way, not a mechanical way.

I guess since my troubled life has been helped many times, I am aware of the many blessings I have received through friends, families, professionals, what spirit guides have put in my path, and so many other happenings, I am clearly aware of.

"What If I Knew", that this was part of my destiny. I doubt life would have been this way thus far, as I would not have strived the way I did. I may not have tried so hard to change, and definitely, I would not have the life and knowledge I have now, or the ability to listen and understand others around me. I don't think I would be as happy as I am.

How do I know I am happy? I try to look at my day, as what was accomplished, what was good in it, and how did the day turn out. I look for the positive, not the negative. I was at one point reminded; do not look at what you did not do, as we all make unattainable lists that way. If we are honest, and see what good we have completed, we are motivated to keep on going. The lists then become accomplishments, and also, our availability to others is more flexible.

Here is where I do Gods work, Gods will, not mine. He gives me the time to help others and finish what really needs to be done on that day I am living. He guides the 24 hour day I am living right now. God also provides for me, through helpful spirit guides. They are specific to the tasks that are destined to be mine in God's great plan. In turn I give my day for God, my will to him, I surrender worry for the tomorrows, or the past, to clear my emotions, my mind, to calm my being, enough to hear, see, and sense what it is I am being guided to do.

In this way of behaving in my waking day, I have time for play, when needed, time for creativity, the way I know I can be, and time to spend with those I love, and time to spend with the me I love, and improve me, by releasing resentments, fears, anger, and jealously. Something I can do in return for the good things I have in life. Thus keeping me from a troubled feeling. This is a reward I am given for my devotion.

So, what about "What If I Knew", I think if I am to be aware of anything, it is likely that I should be aware of my thinking process. How I allow myself to react to those around me, not to be judgmental, or insensitive. I need to know, that I am to be caring, considerate, open minded, tolerant, and accepting.

I must be generous in what I say to boost the morale of another, especially, at a time when they are truly trying hard to improve themselves.

I know that there are different stages in life. They leave all of us at one time or another, feeling awkward, or unsure of how to be around others.

Some of those stages are very fragile times, and can destroy the motivation of a person, to be the best they can be, just by saying something, that may hurt or injure they're fragile sense of being.

So what if I knew, that what I say to a 13 year old girl could give her mixed feelings about her own self esteem, later on in life, may destroy her potential to be her best. What if I knew, what I say to that young man with a half baked idea, makes him forge ahead mindlessly and stubbornly go ahead with the idea, only to mess up any potential in his ideas of the future. That one bad outcome destroys his capable reputation.

I know if you feed a positive attitude the right way, the outcome is beneficial to all and no one losses.

So I guess what I am saying here, is, I have the capability to know a lot without actually knowing everything. Just by how I conduct myself with others. I can't be selfish, and think the world revolves around me, but I can think that I revolve with the world, in a smooth motion of positive thoughts, beings, and

deeds, whether it is my job or just life in general that I am living. Wow, what if I knew this and ignored this. And, wow, I think I just realized that all these thoughts came in a rush, in the moment and time of a red light.

What if I knew this could be how spirit communicates to me, and to all of us. I guess I know it after all, and that is what I have to know, simply and clearly, nothing difficult in understanding this. Spirit really does not take up much of our time in living, but it sure adds to the good time we are living each day.

"As they say seek and ye shall receive", it is the gift God gives us.

Power Powerless
Healing and Purification

There is a word in Najaho "hozhoni"
It means
"Harmony, peace, beauty, balance. "

A balanced harmony between man and nature is strength, being at ease in life, not producing dis-eased. Out of balance becomes weakness (less power), it occurs when man forces or pushes against natural ways.

For example by introducing an unnatural habitat into a natural habitat: Like trying to put a crocodile into a desert land and a chicken into the everglade lands, neither is likely to survive against the laws of nature.

It is good to note, that the Native American used to say, "Why take by force, what can be received or obtained by love and patience. Why destroy what is naturally supplied on this earth?" These are questions that can be asked of us today when weakness or unbalance begins to occur.

Another way of looking at this statement is to think about God being our Great Spirit and creator. God has spirits to work with him, and below him working with us the living being on this earth, our physical world.

Spirit works with natural laws of the universe and Mother Nature. I in other words should be living and doing that same thing, in obtaining what I need, want, and desire. I must think about how I carry out my purpose in life. Do I do it with lies, deceit, or betrayal? With promises made with little or no intent of fulfilling? Is my intent to only take what I want no matter the cost?

These costs could be others being injured or hurt unnecessarily, possibly even killed as in war based on greed, or careless thought of safety and well being. Beauty made or destroyed unnaturally, a lack of sharing causing unneeded suffering for others. Natural laws compromised or broken cause a shift in nature that can devastate. I am aware of cause and effect, a chain reaction resulting from my own actions.

Sometimes I see a vision of what I want, but neglect to think through the process and behavior I chose to take. Forgetting there is a result that comes from my actions. Thus I may get what I want, plus what result may be unwanted, not just affecting me but those around me. Other times my actions may shift the natural laws resulting in missing the goal completely, due to the altering of universal energy.

Native Americans equate life as a great song, each element in perfect harmony with every other element. It is when this natural balance is upset, that illness, bad harvests, and a failure of the hunt, as well as other human misfortunes occur.

As humans we are witnessing the fact of reckless interference within our eco-system which is leading to unforeseen and possibly catastrophic consequences. The notion of fundamental harmony that we as humans possess goes much deeper than this. The need for balance pertains to every area of life. Natural laws pertain to cause and effect, like attracts like, positive to positive.

To be well is to be in balance within body mind and soul and with relation to our environment and society, our all natural world. We are all a part of a natural world.

A Part of the Circle of Life

If I try to live separate from it then disaster will be inevitable, not as a firm retribution from a judging God, but, because I have sung out of harmony. I need to recognize disharmony and bring calmness with meditation, work toward a centered self, then work to reenter within my environment, and within the whole of life's environment. Find my interconnection with others and the world. Well being individually depends on well being of all.

My universe and even myself as a living being, has energies that I can use, energies that come in many forms and ways. Energies can be manipulated for good or ill, to bring healing or imbalance, a cause to harm. It is based on how it is used.

Medicines are composed of energy elements. Medicine used by a medicine person (Shaman), truly means: it is their ability to work with these energies, to bring balance. They work in the unseen world to restore harmony to the seen world.

Naturopathies, western medicine, or even eastern medicine discoveries are used successfully, because of its natural energies found in its components. The aim is that the energy brings about a natural balance to the ill or unbalanced one. A Medicine person looks into the unseen world to see where the sufferer is out of balance, and then calls on energies, through herbs, natural medicines, or counseling to restore harmony and therefore health.

It is tempting to think modern medicine can explain away what an herb is doing chemically, but not all healing can be explained. When I call on those around me to pray: I also call on my medicine person (shaman), and look towards my spirit guides, my higher power (God), to heal either someone I care about or even myself. Here I must have a true belief and acceptance of what the end result is though. Those so sick it seams hopeless, I pray for, accept healing and the outcome, a peaceful passing, or maybe just maybe a healthy outcome, something known as a miracle, since it can't be explained.

There was someone older and wiser (My father a Reverend), who once said to a group of us "healing is a miracle in slow motion". I believe this, I have had witness to this a few times, and most who know me, also know this.

While a modern view focuses on detailed knowledge of the material world, it is gained at the expense of ignoring the greater spiritual perspective. Stricken with illness, minor or life threatening, is a wake up call for me to look deep within to find where disharmony is residing in me, and causing my dis-ease. In finding this within myself, I can now correct it in an appropriate way.

I am of spirit, mind, and body. Worry or guilt creates disharmony of the mind, but can also cause disharmony of the body. This appears as tension, headaches, symptomatic fatigue. It may manifest in many ways including intense pain or discomfort.

Harmony is as different as each person in our circle of life. The skill to heal by a medicine person (Shaman), or ourselves (as instruments that is), is to see into the unique predicament of the ill and restore to balance so that healing can naturally occur. I on a simple level can do this; simply by a review of what it is I am doing to myself and my environment around me.

The modern day Medicine Person (Shaman) prefers to call themselves a Spiritual Advisor (Wa'na'nee'che'), this conveys the essential role of the Shaman. Helping each individual to meet the challenges of their own life, in a way that maintains harmony and balance, with spirit world and the living world, and the great mysteries that embraces everything created by God. There is no aim to cure symptoms of an illness caused by an imbalance. Instead the goal of healing is to restore balance with the natural harmony of life. Each individual by the way is responsible for their own health by way of living. Thoughts and actions create a change in natural energy and harmony; it is the responses made to a given situation that can create disharmony and imbalance or harmony and balance.

This leads us to personal responsibility. I need to acknowledge and accept this and the results I create. If I do not, it will shift in a ball of energy, rolling through my path of life, faster and stronger than I can handle, possibly causing destruction in my life and possibly those surrounding me.

Only when I am truly ready, honest with myself, and have thought through the possible outcomes of my intended actions, should I move into action, being ready for the possible end results. I may get away with many small things at first, then larger things, and then suddenly the big wall is hit, the ending result could be too big to fix on my own. One that forces me to realize just how much and how big my lies, deceit, and betrayal may have become. The hurt is great both for me as the individual and those around me. It may even end up irreversible; it may cause permanent losses and an unbalance in life's cycle and path. Their may be a long journey back to balance and healing.

I guess the meat of what I am trying to say is: God is my main and only entity of energy, to confide in, discuss with, all our thoughts, wishes, and desires, I might want to say here, my needs (the hardest thing to discover in me). I also have something I must do though; I need to know what it is I have to offer up to work with God to go in the direction of my needs. My strengths, realized gifts/talents I can offer up to God, and to do God's will not mine. Trust in him, I will receive what is deserving or needed in my life path, at the right time and place. I must be sure I can handle what I have requested, and offered to work toward. Or accepting what he gives, that is needed.

In return God shares his gift of spirit guides, and spirit life to work with in my path. He also gave me the gift of communication with the six senses to use, a mind to actually think and process my ideas/wants. I also have a natural instinct, an inner voice to confer with. As I use these gifts, they develop stronger and sharper, heightened, they build on my communication to spirit and to God as I understand him. God created all I have, he did so in a way that it meets my basic needs, and if used properly/wisely, and carefully, with love, trust, and discipline, I can obtain even bigger gifts from God.

I need to remember sharing and doing for others, as I would have done unto me. God's gift of life everlasting creates the spirit world. This was taught and demonstrated to all us by our brother Jesus, a Profit who first taught and demonstrated healing and ability to bring peace and balance in life. This is God's greatest gift to me.

I have been blessed with the ability to communicate with spirit world, as well as having spirit contact in many forms and for many reasons. I even have a gift of being an instrument to offer for spirit use if I accept the opportunity.

Spirit needs me to work through, to give healing energies to restore others to health, physical, mentally, and spiritually, not necessarily in that order, but in those ways. Spirit also communicates in many ways with me, through other people, natural occurrences, and our many developed Medias of communication. In being able to do this, spirit can provide guidance, lessons, inspiration, and wisdom. Which I can utilize to answer my own problems, or lead me to answers I need or seek, as well as creating healing for me.

I need to do something as well, to be able to receive these gifts and blessings though. I need to work continuously for the goodness of my living world, not just my own agendas. I need to develop a manner of communication in which to live. This requires trust, devotion, discipline, and dedication, as well as acceptance of spirits results and outcomes for me individually and as a whole of mankind. Accepting life's challenges and working with spirit to succeed, as well as acceptance of life and death within natural means, life everlasting in a spirit world after the living world.

I also need to live love within me and out towards others, live with a sincere attitude and honesty to self and others. If I live a healthy balanced life style with a sincere honest attitude and action, if it is meant to be, spirit will help and heal me as I request. When I ask, I must also foresee how I will work with the spirit energy I receive, do my part, and with all my heart.

Again this does not mean to give up my western medicine, but to work with what I know I need to do, and do it, and allow spirit the chance to bring healing to me or those I am trying to help. All it takes once again is a willingness to be honest and true in my efforts, an acceptance of changes that must be made by spirit world and I. I must think of what I am asking for and how it may change me and those around me, how it will effect the world around me.

Today is a special day we are blessed with an opportunity of offering up to spirit our request for help and healing through our "Knock down Healing Service. I believe there is no better opportunity than this to present and meet with contact, sprit energy, the light of Jesus Christ invited into us and entering. Participate with a positive attitude, a positively thought out request, and the trust and belief in spirit world, work, and healing. Offer up your part you are willing to play in your request. Remember this is not short term work it is long term, life everlasting.

My first true miracle was the healing of my daughter, whose life was threatened by cancer, slowly she returned to a healthy enjoyable full life, there may be some lingering affects, but she has accepted them, and lives each day with a different view. You can only live life today.

I believe so far the work and healing my son is receiving is also a miracle so far, but, I still accept and so does he, what is best for him, the end result of spirit healing, whether on this the physical world, or full healing on the spirit side. So far he is with us. I cherish the time given each day, and continue to do what I have to do for today, offering my part of living life one day at a time, like it is the only one I have.

May God Bless You All!

Continued Pursuit of Healing

As we all know, I have been pursuing the development of my ability to be an effective healing instrument. This means strengthening my connection with spirit, and be accepting and allowing spirit to work through me for others.

I pursue classes, I read about spirit work to understand it, I practice daily, and meditate daily, so I can be that instrument spirit needs. As I attend church and listen to speakers sharing their own experiences and gained knowledge, I learn much more.

I believe spirit teaches us through others. I accept all opportunities to practice healing; I make it part of my life just as I do breathing, eating, and living. The classes allow me to develop even more, my healing, and recently, I have been changing my life to a more positive, uplifted attitude, and behavior. This means being positive no matter what or who is affecting me in my day. I will not say I am perfect at that, but I am merely changing toward being that way.

I realize and accept that healing is an important part of human survival, it is more than just physical changes, it is emotional (mental), and spiritual (soul).

The main object of being healed is often overlooked. In order for the physical being to be healed, we must ensure that the mental emotional roller coaster we are on is slowed and halted. We need to be willing to make the changes in ourselves that are necessary. That means the way we think, act or behave, and the way we live. We need to find the spiritual self in us, and work on strengthening that as well. This may be the realization, that we must ask for strength and courage to meet the challenge ahead of us to be healed.

Healing takes time as well, it is not just a passing of seconds into relief of our troubles. We often go unwell with out notice for a great deal of time. It takes time to reverse the problems, as well it is just how much is put into the healing, and we have to figure out what is the cause, and change that. If it is a way of living problem, it may take time and effort to change that, habits are hard to break, but not impossible. We also have to accept that some things, may never be healed, or may only be healed once crossing over to spirit life. I don't want to say that to discourage anyone, but, sometimes accepting dying and life after death, deep in our soul, is what is needed for the healing to occur. Being willing and accepting of death is the only thing you may be able to do, and live life for today only and nothing more. We need the spiritual awakening to happen, for healing to take place.

Healing must come from within our selves. All healing is first accomplished on an inner spiritual level, and is shown on the outer physical body (if needed) later. There is a need to be open and accepting with belief and trust from deep within us, being receptive to the healing vibrations of spirit.

Now that is somewhat a summary of what I have learned, and experienced in life so far. I have had to learn how to deal with the rollercoaster's of emotions, it is a constant effort. I seek to learn how to cope with very real fears and distress, brought on by personal events. Learning to let go of what I cannot do without help. Learning to face tasks that need to be done, to remove the stress and fear, and not running away from anything.

Actual living is a lesson constant and ongoing. I need to develop a manner of positive living, positive affirmations, positive thinking and doing. Define what I really want out of life, revisiting that and evaluate how things are going toward that. Realize its importance, and the affect it has on me as I continue to move toward the goals. Does it bring me closer to my ultimate goal of happiness, comfort, and serenity? Will my wants make me happy or stressed, emotionally twisted, or strong? Or will they bring me a greater spiritualality, more meaningful personal relationships, improved living and wellbeing.

In an effort to define and obtain, am I really setting realistic goals, or setting my self up for failure as I can often do. I have to realize that what is positive, and what I think is positive may be two different things, when trying to force a desire to happen.

Negative thoughts beings or deeds are produced in frustration and greed, jealousy, or envy. This is what needs to be recognized and realized, then avoided, or dismissed from us. This is when there is a need to rebalance and regroup my energies. There is this saying, "as a human thinks, so shall he be." So I must think positive and be positive, utilize the positive, and draw the positive into me, and around me. Like attracting like as is said.

An exercise I did at one point in life was to carry a notebook, and in it I made notes of certain feelings and behaviors, and the affect it was having in my day, and path. I did it for a month or so, within a few days though I noted how often I was negative, or ill thinking, and it was a surprise, as the weeks went though these things became fewer, because I didn't like what was in the note book. I needed and wanted to change that.

Who wants to be thought of as negative, sour, or someone to avoid. I saw flaws, the perfectionist, critic, stubborn, and sometimes aggressive. I didn't like it too much, but, seeing is believing, and changing it, comes easier. I may mean well, but that doesn't mean I am always right, and certainly, not qualified to judge the other person, but I can love and send love, think positive, model positive, and it rubs off, and attracts.

A journal helps to revamp yourself, clean away and shine the attributes you have, believe it or not those negatives can be positive if used properly. Stubborn for example can end up being tolerance to communicate, and patience to be understood, or to understand. Balance can be produced, and a realization of potential can be uncovered and worked towards.

In improving your life, it opens you to greater spiritual contact, increasing spiritual energy, and reception of spirit communication and healing. Whatever you activate becomes the energy you have, be positive and act positive, and life is positive. Put a positive shield around you and you can not be harmed. Have faith in your spirit guides. Ask them to help and protect you, they will, the key though is trust, belief, and acceptance.

Opening your heart and mind with a love energy is the start. Once you are able to do this, loving yourself, will lead you to hear things differently, you will interpret things differently, and certainly spirit will communicate with you and heal. You may hear a message that feels good inside, or feel a good energy from someone that feels better. Maybe you will go to someone you think can help you heal, and you will feel it you will know it, because you are open to it.

Only good spirits will work with you, because you will not accept a negative energy any more. Spirit will walk alongside you, feel their vibration, and they will communicate and protect you. The way you reach that meeting place of healing, depends on the path you walk, and how you walk it. If it feels good, and you are happy in it, then it will continue. As long as you are comfortable within your life and can live with you, healing can occur.

No one else determines your life destination, only you do, spirit will help, but will not direct an answer to you. They will be there to keep you safe from harm, but now you will have to learn how to work with your spirit guides, and help yourself in life's lessons.

That is another topic, to be discussed, but one you can search on your own as well, just ask a Spiritualist and they will be happy to walk with you seeking the lessons. Have a happy pathway, God Bless you.

My Walk My Talk with God

It was a wonderful Easter weekend that I took off for a long awaited break from the world. I had had a few busy weeks, many things to deal with, and many things that I needed to just let go of in my heart and mind. I went to one of my favorite places for my break. Inverness Falls, in the Big Whiteshell. The rugged beauty of the landscape just attracts me, and brings me down to earth, grounded and relaxed. I looked forward to just resting, walking, hiking, photography, and most of all more writing opportunities. The drive alone gets me relaxed, and when I can't get away, I do just think about the travels I have had, it is so nice and relaxing.

I took my hiking in parts over that weekend; I hadn't done much hiking for a while so I thought I should pace myself. In my hiking it was new and different, of course all are different in what I get from them, but this one was new in energy and affirmations for me. I tend to meditate while walking, hard to explain, but in those walks I have me, my heart, my spirit, and God's spirit energy with me. I get thoughts, and hear what spirit tries to tell me, but I don't hear in the chaos of my mind when things are tough.

The first day I hiked through Inverness Falls. It was a gorgeous day. I set out by the falls backpack full of camera's of different sorts, and an anxious mind. I had an added bonus for the hike. A white dog; belonging to the owners of the resort. This dog had one blue eye, and one brown eye, very beautiful. She was playful and friendly. She walked with me on my hike all the way I might add. She would run up ahead of me, then come back and meet me up the path. She was a great hiking companion; no complaining, no chatting on and on, peaceful, friendly assistive in my trek, playful, just what I needed. I felt it was a gift in a sense, from God, we didn't know each other, but we got to know each other. The views were beautiful, my thoughts wandered. I would stop at various spots for pictures. I thought about times in the past; what I felt I had lived through, and what my family had lived through as well. I felt a great sense of energy from the thoughts and heard a voice that said "And you have survived it, your children too have survived. All your family has taken the challenges in stride. Each has become stronger and wiser in the scheme of things."

I thought about this and realized each time it was asked, strength and guidance has come to me, and others. When the challenge seemed too much or too big, I realized I did not say I can't do it, instead I always seemed to ask for strength and guidance to meet the challenges. I have never really asked to just have challenges I think I can handle, which would minimize my life experience greatly, I suppose.

On My walk I saw a water fall that rushed through and over the rocks. The current was strong and fast. I noticed the water flowed over the rocks, but under the frozen ice. It never went over the ice, just under the ice. Mother Nature was at work. If the water went over the ice it would likely freeze and the ice would get thicker on top, and block the flow. All natures' wonders would continue to have water as needed. It came to me then in thought that sometimes we have to go under the current of troubles, especially when they are not meant to be ours to work with in our path of life. Trouble may enter my path, but, I must remember, it may have entered with someone else in my path. I can extend a hand of support and strength for that individual, but I don't have to have the answer. They will find their own answer in time. I may be just the current of strength they may need. What a great thought, with strength and wisdom in it. It was not just words, it was images, impressions, refreshing new energy, and it came together in a package from my walk and talk with spirit and God.

I walked on with my hike, dog in tow. I was going well on the trail, but, I decided to step off the trail a bit. I wanted a perfect picture of some scenery I saw. Well wouldn't you know it, I was a few steps off the path and sunk up to my waist in snow. Of course the dog thought I was playing, or I thought the dog wanted to play with me, I am not sure. She licked my face, jumped and pranced all around me. She panted and I swear I think I saw her laugh. I ended up hearing "go off the path and find trouble, get back on the path, brush yourself off (snow is cold) and laugh. I just learned a lesson of why your path is leading you the way it is. Don't fight it. I dug myself out and got back on the path and carried on, while kind of chuckling to myself.

I carried on, again thinking about what is going on in my life, mostly good stuff, but a few sad or not so nice thoughts. As I came around a bend in my hiking trail I saw a poplar tree growing in the strangest direction. It was bent in a bowing manner, just like a rainbow. Well again I hear a voice in me say......"Mother Nature has to bend at times too, to get through the difficulties of following natural laws." I thought to myself isn't mother nature also law? I heard in me these spirit voices again answer, "Natural Law follows universal energy and law." "Mother nature also is a part of natural laws. Even she has to bend at times to survive and meet the challenges of natural law." I too must remember this and accept it. It is okay for me to bend at times when growth, direction, and change occur. All this from a poplar bent out of shape.

I carried on and reached the peak of the hike, a rock bluff over looking a wetland bed of frozen reeds and bulrushes, upright frozen in snow and ice. The yellows and browns looked very nice. I had made it beyond the point that I could go (you see I hadn't been out hiking or walking much the past few years). I made it a bit out of breath, but feeling invigorated all the same. I was feeling good, I stopped to rest and do a small meditation; I do this when ever I hike and stop to rest. I gave thanks for all I had in my spiritual, mental, and physical life. I see it as, I could do what I do because of my faith and belief in God and spirit life. The changes I have made, devotion, and discipline, I give to my spiritual life have given me more riches in life, I hadn't been able to see at one time. Well I hiked it back for the day, back to my cabin. A fire built and a quiet evening in, reflecting on my day, then off to sleep.

The next day I took off on another trail, a little less difficult but longer. It was so nice and warm. A bright sun, a warm breeze, and a wonderful feeling. I didn't have my buddy with me that day, I was on my own. I saw all these cabins along the way, everyone out doing something in this beautiful day. A day not to be wasted indoors. I walked the curves and bends, the inclines and declines of the path, it was so refreshing, and at one point I saw something that surprised me.

As my thoughts were on the recent trouble my son was having in hospital, I found myself arguing with myself. Here I am on sabbatical because I need it, and I was feeling guilty that I wasn't there to visit and maybe change the outcome of the incident (that being getting punched by another patient). I then corrected my thinking. My kids were not toddlers anymore, they are adults, they get hurt, and it isn't up to me to cushion their falls, prevent injuries, or spare hurt feelings (Oh, but I really would like to). I need to let go, and let them live their own lives.

Experience life, mistakes or great gains, but, all of life. I am a mother and always will be, I can offer support and strength at this time in life and that is it. Bailing them out, always interfering with my suggestions of directions really would not help. Sharing my experience in life but not my opinions of directions is okay. My mind and that voice conversing on my reflections, as we passed another moment by, there in my sights were two poplar trees on the path. They were criss-crossing themselves.................. hmmm crossing-crosses.

Okay I heard what was impressed, "we all have our crosses to bear. " "We don't bare others, but we can walk with them, and lend support and strength. We just aren't supposed to carry someone else's cross. Who knows, if we take it, it weights us down and of course the cross they had may be replaced with a harsher more challenging cross, as we all live in a life path, a life journey."

We need to meet and master certain challenges to learn and experience life. We gain our strength, wisdom, and serenity when meeting the challenges in our own life. To take away that responsibility is to remove opportunity for the individual it was meant for.

Okay I get it. I also realized it is okay to feel sad for what each of my kids have endured in their young lives, but they have survived so far, and they are stronger for it, even wiser for it. My son may have a path that challenges him right now, but, he is alive, he is not in jail, he is being looked after, in more ways than one. God, spirit, and humanity are kind and generous to him, and he is making good progress. To a point of surprising me with calling home and talking to me. There was a time; I never imagined this could happen.

My oldest is getting on track in life after her own challenges, and what seemed like insurmountable odds against her, many times in her short life so far. My middle child informed they were moving, the house was sold, and they have a new home in the country, just like that, over night all said and done. I was surprised and thought wow, my daughter and son-in-law are making major decisions, on their own.

She explained her reasons and rationales, all sound and good, very grounded. This from the child that would runaway from home, from stress or serious decisions. She has really grown up and has made a good start in life. She works hard and is very loving and understanding. She is loyal and devoted to family, friends, and co workers.

Wow! I just got the feeling of pride for my family and a lift of weight off my shoulders. Look after my own cross and well being, and I will be of use to help others in a way of Gods will not mine.

So at the cross roads of the path I am on, I am shown natures cross in the form of two poplars, the kind of tree I here from others are useless annoying trees, Guess they are wrong. A poplar taught me its okay to bend a bit, if going with the flow of natural law. A small waterfall taught me nature's way of continuing on in natural law, and two more poplars taught me to carry my own cross, and not others, but to be supportive of others. So poplars in life suddenly have purpose, so do all of us at some point of the journey in life.

All I can say is thanks, to my guides, and other spirit beings that came into my life, and so did God, I invited them; but, I think they would have come along no matter what. So what I have learned is when I take a walk, I get to have a good talk between God, my guides, and I.

Good Bless

When you do for others, they do not learn to do for themselves, and so you rob them of their self-esteem.

Bye the way, the Dogs name was Serenity.

Reading from the Greber Bible
Mathew Chapter 22
Verses 36 – 39

Master, which is the great commandment in the Law?
Jesus said unto him thou shalt love the lord thy God with
all thy heart, with all thy soul and, with all thy mind.
Thou shalt love thy neighbor as thyself. This
is the second commandment.

"Invite Balance and Harmony"

Putting together readings of inspiration are very hard at times to do. It takes plenty of time and devotion to tune out the world, and meditate quietly. In all my writings, I have found it difficult to start, or to put the thoughts together and making sense. When my thoughts do start to flow, there is more than just my own. I find myself connected to a world of spiritual inspiration and communications.

You may think this sounds a bit nutty, but, I am sharing, what I truly have received from my higher power and spirit guides. It is up to those reading to accept or ignore, but even if you find this hard to take, read and see if it inspires you or gives some answer to questions you have about life and your path in it. The question I had before the writing was "Where am I at in my spiritual beliefs and way of living?"

It is no secret that we all have ups and downs in our lives, definitely I am in that roller coaster presently. So what is it I can do to bring or restore balance and harmony in my living world right now?

Am I on my paths journey solidly or is it sketchy? How do I perceive things at present? I know I have felt frustration, disappointment, dissatisfaction recently with where I am at. So what am I doing about it? Where is it I think I want to head for? In asking myself this, I thought of a few places to seek my answers.

First off I live a program based on spirituality and twelve simple steps to follow. I have the help of many tools to follow this, not everyone has this program though, I am glad I have it. If I didn't have this program I thought well I could seek other outlets to gain balance physically, mentally and spiritually.

My second thought was, I belong to a church which teaches and leads me in living spiritually. A church that can provide guidance, lessons, fellowship, love, and a family community, just to name a few of its benefits.

As a church it provides an example of living spiritually. I have learned much about myself as a person, and what I have to offer in my daily living.

I also have been learning what it takes to become a medium, thus helping others with spirit communications. As well I am learning about becoming a healer, something I enjoy and get much satisfaction in doing, because it gives me an opportunity to work with others and help others.

The Spiritualist Church has offered me a chance to receive healing for mind, body, and soul. It has also offered myself and others a chance to attend classes, and develop my spiritual self, the gifts I may have, and the ability to use them for the betterment of mankind, that being those around me and coming in contact with me; also the ability to increase my personal contact with spirit world at the highest and best possible level.

I have learned about spiritual principles, which is believed and followed by all members of the church. I strive daily to live by them. Some days and some principles may seem harder than others, but in reviewing why: it seems it may be due to my own personal interference with the flow of energy at that time. You see I know the principles and have somewhat of a basic understanding, but I must continually seek further knowledge and understanding of the same.

Now recognizing that part of my being, I decided to look further at what else I can do to improve my living and purpose of living. I thought well we have natural laws that we can follow, so where I am at with knowing and understanding these. When I set out to research then I found there are many, and if really thought about, the list could be as endless as nature itself. There are many ways of viewing natural laws and how it affects all areas of one's life.

The natural laws if understood and followed can bring about changes and growth in love, success of the working life, healing, and health, spiritual contact and growth to name but a few. There are so many laws that the list could go on forever, so I've decided I will have to learn daily about each as they are experienced through my daily living. Some of these laws are basic and understandable these are;

Law of belief/desire
Law of receptivity
Law of cooperation
Law of love
Law of mind

Law of vibration
Law of cause and effect
Law of oneness
Law of harmony
Law of gratitude

As I have said these are just a few to start with. When we start to live within these few laws, we are starting a spiritual life path, bringing together sound mind, body, and spirit.

If I can build my spiritual awareness, I can build the strengths I need to go through life, balanced, healthy, and satisfied. As a student I have learned a lot about spiritual awareness. I have made many notes in class on my responsibilities as a student to work on spiritual awareness. As you work to build such awareness you also grow as a medium. Something I decided early on that I wanted to be. So looking back in my massive amounts of notes, periodicals, and The few books I have, I researched how I could continually build as a medium through increased spiritual awareness, thus improving my daily living as well. Here are some of the steps spirits and I have come up with

Live My Own Life

> "I grow as I exercise my faculties! "Expression" Is a necessary form of spiritual exercise! I must for the need of myself, live my own life!" (Sermonettes- an Interpretation of Spiritualism- Joseph P. Whitwell)

Of lately, I have been drawn to the thoughts of being rich, and what we would do with a large windfall of money. Sad to say, but easy also, "So I didn't win the 6-49." Work is for the worker.

This was a thought, an inspiration while I shoveled away the heavy snowfall from Monday. I spent the better part of Tuesday clearing the snow. As did the rest of Winnipeg I would say. I shoveled all that beautiful white stuff, thinking however, that the person who did win, I knew and she was a very nice person to boot. I was happy for her, so I smiled at the thought. I kept shoveling. Then more thoughts came to me. Why of course you've got it, my next inspired writing and talk.

I didn't win the lottery, because I have all this ability and talent that should not be wasted. I mean look at me I am able to shovel. Why do I have to shovel, what motivates me? There are obvious reasons, but here are my thoughts on it.

One reason is so I do not have to trudge through deep snow in my yard.

Second, my car was buried; I couldn't drive it if I didn't clear the snow. Hmmm, that's right I own a car! It is mine as long as I make my payments. I can use it however I see fit to use it. However it does come with responsibility.

Thirdly; I am able to work at home. My clients need to be able to safely come to the door. I also am able to work at a school part time, and a clinic on occasional days for consult work. All of which I totally enjoy doing.

Fourthly; Big thought, I own my own home, it is warm and secure, comfortable and sound. It comes with responsibilities as well, but I at least have something to work for.

Fifthly; now here I strayed a bit in thought, but it came this way. I have my intellect; I can learn and do many things in life, it is my choice. I have a good education and I am a skilled nurse and reflexologist. Yes I had to study and work hard for it, but, it was my choice to develop this path of life. This comes with responsibility. I have to maintain and increase my knowledge and skills professionally and personally. That is why I still attend university and training seminars, which again is a privilege. All this allows me a secure but modest income, but still very good and comfortable.

Sixthly; I have my health and physical strength, it has its limitations, but none the less allows me to do necessary things for my good and welfare. If I am unable to do for myself, I am able to hire and pay for someone to assist or do for me those tasks. My responsibility is to budget my finances to cover needs, and look after my fitness and health on a daily basis. Now these are just a few of the many thoughts I had after saying to myself, "So I didn't win the lottery."

As I shoveled, it was not all gratitude I had, but, none the less I counted my blessings and was accepting of my personal responsibility in life. So I didn't win the money to finance a world tour, nor the vision of donations to worthy charities and causes I believe in. If I budget carefully, I am able to make financial donations as well. I would be able to do this humbly without ego boosting grandiose grand standing of a financial windfall. That was a fancy mouthful.

To quote Joseph P. Whitwell, "As the fruit tree demonstrates its value by bearing fruit given from within, so also does man demonstrate his worth to his kind by those things which comes forth from within."

Honestly it is nice to fantasize but there is a need to keep grounded in reality and accept the hand dealt and work with it. I am lucky; at least that is how I see it. I have a good relationship with my higher power and spirit world. I do not work totally alone and it is not with my will, but it is with God's will and plan I work within.

I may not have much to offer, but each day I arise, I offer my day to God and spirit world. I offer my best 100%, and I do my best. There is no hesitation or restrictions to my offering.

I am thankful; my life is rich in many ways. Yes I have had some sad and rough moments in life, but, I choose not to wade or wallow through it lingering on. I accept and get busy with a positive attitude, so not to have a foggy path. Pity clouds reality, judgment, and direction in which I am meant to go.

I can count the many struggles I have endured, but my list of what I have doesn't seem to end, or come to a total tally, as things are still coming. It will not end as long as I keep looking and accepting what is to come. My responsibility is to develop and prepare myself for what I am needing in life and hoping to receive in life.

I choose to live in a giving manner. Not to give away all I have or to martyr myself, but to give as in sharing my richly gains, physically, spiritually, emotionally and yes even financially at times. I try to do this in a manner of thinking; I am rich and blessed and have much to share. The more I share the richer I am, because I continue to receive. I do this without expectation from those I share with. It is the good will I feel in my heart and soul; it is in knowing that one less person does not do without. It feels good to smile and receive a smile back for instance, instead of receiving a glare in return for my smile.

This is a very simple example of what I mean. I seek to see what it is I can do to create a positive atmosphere for myself and others around me.

I have common sense enough to know a positive attitude and way of life is a better way to journey in life.

I have knowledge of spirit, spirit work, and spirit world. I trust and believe in the ability to work with spirit and spirits abilities to heal and alter negative to positive in life. I may have abilities that have been developed, but I also know I can be an instrument through which spirit can work and do many things. I only need to be willing and able to work with spirit. My responsibility and choice to do so require further lessons and studies, learning as well as discipline and devotion in a way of life necessary of me for spirit work to happen.

Spirit guides and directs us
Heals and strengthens us
Brings loving energy and encouragement
Speaks to us in many different ways
Teaching and enlightening us

I grow as I exercise my faculties
Expression is a necessary form of spiritual exercise
I must for the need of myself live my own life
Work is for the worker
I am responsible for my own path and richness

Thank you Dr. Silvers and Spirit helpers
God Bless.

A Soul's Life

The soul is immortal, it is as important as the mind
It should be guarded and protected at all costs
What ever happens to it in the this living world
Will determine where it shall start in the afterlife

In the afterlife our soul will face the truth
How it was that we lived and what we experienced
There is no hell or heavenly kingdom
There is no magical cleansing of the soul in afterlife

What we live now determines where
we will start in the afterlife
What we do now determines what we
may need to do in the afterlife
We gain wisdom with experience good or bad in life
How we handle life now prepares us for the afterlife

There is no hell or heaven in a sense of place after death
In our living world, how we act or respond
Determines the level of good or bad, that results in our lives
If we don't complete our purpose in life, we are
given time to complete in the afterlife

In our physical world our soul brings joy and authenticity
It is the creativity and inner love and peace
Our soul is the immaterial essence of our inner being
It is the drive of life, the emotion and spirit of our mind

The soul may suffer illness if the mind,
body, and spirit are unbalanced
We need be careful to not loose touch with
our true self, direction, and intention
Remember the meaning of life for you
Or you may loose the connection with your soul

When you may find then that you are
unable to connect with others or self
Feeling out of rhythm, harmony, or profoundly lonely with self
It is the soul's essence that signals us when not
being true to self or forgotten life's purpose
Whether trauma, emotional loss, physical
illness, or unsatisfied relations

The soul is a part of our being, helping us feel alive
Reaching down into the bones, awakens
us to goodness and gifts within us
The soul is the quality of our consciousness, our inner being
A spirit that which is transcendent and takes us beyond self

The soul is life energy and part of a greater life force
That which connects us to others,
communities, nature, and the divine
Family, friends, environment, and spirit all influence the soul
Our purpose is to share the souls grace
as its essence has no boundaries

Open a dimension to experience life and self
with depth, heart, and fellowship
Make contact with your soul in prayer,
meditation, and creativity
It will awaken and speak out the true nature of you
Dream, fantasize, and create with prayer

Communicating with the mind, spirit,
and body reaching the soul
Imagination gives us joy, hope, and pleasure
It invents solutions to problems or needs
Both medicine for the soul and a wellness practiced
It creates new ways of seeing and being in the world
It often takes an abrupt change in life circumstances
To lead us to its reparative powers and strength
The dark night of the soul that brings us to find a healing path

It is a quest to recover one's soul rarely cautiously planned
You may awaken one day to find you suffer a loss
Deep to you, you reach to understand and
you realize your own mortality
There must be a meaning from what
has impacted my inner being

Your journey in life, experience gained, the
deeper understanding apparent
It is what creates the realization that
what you feel is the connection
From your minds thoughts, to your soul's inner essence
This is the life of your soul, the everlasting life
infinite, powerful, God's light energy

We must guard this soul of ours
Take care of the temple which houses it
Allow love from within to flow outward from the heart
Give thought through our mind, not just our
brain, life's path the journey always blessed

God Bless and thank you to my guides

Holistic Fitness

As a nurse my training days were molded on a thought that the total some of all parts of the being must be balanced, fully functioning, and in harmony together. That being said, I as a student nurse was taught that the mind, the body, and the spiritual parts of our lives affected one another, and, all would need to be in working order for the fulfillment of total health benefits. So you may hear some familiar thoughts from one of my previous talks and one that was shared with us a few weeks ago, by Gloria.

Like I was saying as a nurse I had to take into consideration, the patients state of mind, their physical status, and as well the spiritual state of health. Yes I did say state of health of the spiritual aspect of the patient.

That last part being a difficult one to assess at times. I know that with each culture, each heritage traditions, and each religious background, there are many things to consider for an individual patient.

Luckily, I am only going to base my assessment on spiritualism in this talk, and a spiritualist's level of health. As spiritualists we believe that all is God. Our divine being resides inside our hearts and minds as our psyche, our soul. Because we are of a psyche in nature, the soul is never fully in our conscious awareness. The soul is only partially revealing truth. Thus we work to open ourselves exploring within our self to find our beliefs, our knowledge of reality, and our interpretation of what we perceive to be real. That is the content within our heart, our soul, our spirit of being. This being stated, what is it we need to provide a healthy well being of our spirit being? How do we stay fit spiritually?

Physically we now that a balance of exercise, diet, and rest, keep us in shape for ability to survive. We see our doctors when not feeling physically well, and we do the right things to repair any damages to our physical being.

Mentally we know it is important to keep the mind balanced too. In this case it takes the proper amount of rest, exercising it with knowledge and sorting things out that bother us, as well as thinking things through to make healthy decisions. Our mind needs the right amount of rest and relaxation, freedom to express creativity and ideas, as well as and not limited to a stable manor of living, which includes keeping up with our personal responsibilities, business demands, financial stability, a stable relationship with those around us, taking personal responsibility for our thoughts and actions.

Spiritually we need to know how we feel about having a higher power, A God of our understanding, as spiritualists we need to understand the world of spirit and how it works for us and with us. Are we ok with the idea of spirit beings and the communication that we receive. Are we willing to accept spirits help, in our way of living? Are we doing all we can to reach a harmonized spiritual being for ourselves? If we think we are not quite where we want to be with our spiritual life, do we know what we need to do to get there?

How many times have we listened to a sales pitch for a product promising weight loss and a healthier body image? Take note though, that the gimmick also requires and states in small print, in conjunction with proper diet and exercise. Maybe we should save any money there and just do a few sit ups and walks in our day, and eat proper. My thoughts for myself these days are.... I can keep my financial stability while getting some rest, exercise, and proper diet, by doing it myself. The same goes for all those other beauty promises, age defying creams and potions, live healthy, and you will be healthy.

Recently I saw a paid advertisement program, it was trying to sell the viewer on miracle water, and it was oxygenated and held real healing powers, well Dah.... Water has oxygen, thus the chemical H2O, with the pitch they threw in some hallelujahs, and bible quotes, this hinted to me, belief in prayer helps too, it also got me thinking, it improves your workouts and it's affects, well if my attitude was positive going into exercising, maybe tap water might be just as good.

Now onto emotional fitness=mental fitness. Again, this is a no brainer, sorry.... No pun intended. Get out and clear your thoughts, put things in perspective, face fears, budget time, get control of anger and resentment, these will exhaust your mind almost instantly. Settle worries, anxiety, panic by removing the mitigating circumstances. Guess what, these and other common sense things are easier than you think to do, as long as you are honest and true about what you can do for the problem, and put it into action immediately. Accept help when it is offered, you never know where it may come from, but, if you are willing to accept help, spirit will put things in place to help you. But, remember spirit is not there to bail you out of repeat mistakes, you must also learn from your experiences.

If work gets you down, ask yourself why this is, and give an honest look at it, be honest with yourself. Are you too negative at times, or does someone draw you into a negative environment? Is it a difficulty with the tasks assigned, or is it because you do a job that does not give you satisfaction or a good feeling? Why did you want this job, for money and material gains only, or because you did at one time like it, but have forgotten why you did like it? Change the negative to positive, if someone is negative, don't get into it, just remove yourself and stay positive. No solution is easy, and really in life nothing comes free or easy, that is worth having.

Now the big third part of healthy living and life's balance the spiritual aspect of life. How healthy do you think you are in this area of life? We are not talking about how often you attend a church or show outwardly to others you are a spiritual person. To be spiritual, it has to be within you a part of you, like breathing is. Church offers a time of paying respect, reflection, and a source of hope, help, love, as well as community belonging. Like this talk, may help someone find an answer that was there already, but may not have been recognized if not for listening to another persons take on life. Believe me; I hope someone gets something from my talks. I know I do because I journey with my guides, and listen within, what may be given to me for guidance and understanding. My higher power has given me gifts to use to help myself and others, I also have spirit helpers that I try always to listen to for guidance and knowledge of what God's great plan is for me.

Spiritual fitness is; Loving from within outwardly, Giving, having tolerance, acceptance, living in peacefulness, and serenity.

Church helps you to understand, it helps you and those around, by bringing everyone together for a meeting of cohesiveness and healing. It provides guidance, sets examples, opens a social door, and should be satisfying and stimulating positive energy and vibrations.

Spiritual fitness should be a way to connect with your higher power as you understand it, on a daily and constant way. When spiritually fit you should be able to find guidance, direction, and energy to do what needs to be done. The ability to feel like you are being healed as you make your journey in life. If things are tough, then why, is there a lesson to learn, or an experience needed for you to go through for a future time to help others when they need it?

So what should be the way to a healthy spiritual life?

Try to find peace in your day, make peace with others, and let it go, whether they are willing to make peace or not, it is you that needs to feel you have done so.

Think things through, don't just rush into things that need time and thought, be sure you are able to do what is required in your day. Take time to feel guidance in your daily living, it is not my will but God's will that you need to remember. In connecting with spirit and God you may hear, feel, or sense what it is you need to be doing. You will find answers quicker and better if you allow spirit to help. Sometimes rushing into things is the worst idea, especially if your heart is not into it. Think with your heart and mind together, the right one will guide you.

Now working with God and spirit is not a quick learn thing. It takes time and devotion with out any stipulations or limitations to the time and manner of the answers. It takes a strong inner self, one that does not give in to what goes against your ethical moral being. Be true to yourself always, and be comfortable and able to live with your inner self. Be authentic not what you think others want to see in you.

Spiritual Reflections

Being spiritual requires self honesty, and reflection/evaluation of self. You need to work at it constantly, and be disciplined in your way of living. In time much of this becomes automatic just like moving and breathing. Never compromise your beliefs or moral ethics.

One needs to have a willingness to learn about spirit world, spiritual living and understanding.

When you are feeling down or week in some way, there are ten questions to ask yourself.

1. Check in with self, do an assessment of what is troubling you.

2. Move a muscle, change a thought, sometimes it is merely a misunderstood thought you may be having.

3. Plan a surprise, maybe you just haven't used up your creative energy, and there may be someone out there that needs a lift.

4. Smile pretty, or pleasantly, everyone will wonder what you are up to and you won't have to say anything, they will smile back at you, which when you think of it may be all that is missing for you at that moment.

5. Boost your happy hormone, check your diet, you may be missing something in nutrients at the moment.

6. Halt, are you Hungry, Angry, or Lonely, or are you just Tired? You may need to care for one or more of these things.

7. Get out of self, find out what others are doing, maybe you are lacking the social aspect in living.

8. Get active, a lack of stimuli or energy use can be a downer on its own.

9. Are you having your own pity party, never party alone, and never have a negative party, be honest with yourself is life that bad for you, count your blessings.

10. Are you in a pout mode, then stop it, I can tell you one thing about pouting, people can tell you lost the battle when you pout. Also most people have no sympathy or empathy for a pouter; no one likes to ruin a good day with a negative energy.

So be good to yourself, do good, be good to others, and live a good orderly direction and there you will find God, and a spiritual way of life, to add to your whole being.

As a nurse I work with all my clients/patients in a holistic way, thus I am able to heal in more ways than one for my clients.

God Bless and have a happy 24 hours.

You Are Not Walking Alone…..

If you have been swept off your feet lately, then get on your knees and say thank you, if it creates joy in your life or…..

Say Great Spirit Lord guide me through, if you are overwhelmed at what life is throwing at you, or giving you to deal with.

Just when is it we are walking with our spirit brother Jesus. When we choose to or when we are clearly aware we need guidance. If we know we never walk alone in our daily walk of life; why is it we catch ourselves at times ignoring the Great Spirit we walk with and usually talk to.

I know if I went hiking or walking with other people, I would be hard pressed to ignore them, before they would make me aware of the lack of communication. I would be asked what's wrong. Are you upset? What's got your attention so deep you are not paying any attention to us?

We don't go out with others and then totally ignore them while we are with them, without a good reason at least……or do we…….strange behavior if we do! We all know the verses of "Foot Prints" Jesus carries us in troubled times, when we ask him to, this is the same as with Spirit. We are never left to struggle on our own no matter the trouble or burden. I would hope we all believe this, and accept this idea.

So when, why, where, for what reason, and whom to we talk to and walk with in life? For me, I include all of this into the concept of communicating with spirit, God, or even nature, on a daily basis. I awake and start my day this way; I frequent this idea through the day, and at the end of my day.

At home I hum along and work with my higher power and

spirit helpers, to provide healing in all the work and connections with others I encounter through the day. At my Work outside the home the same goes. In my free time, going for walks, hiking, photography, flea market hunting, and many other joys, and tasks. Anything I do, I offer myself as an instrument to do my best to be guided to do what is good for all. I have fun, and feel connected and safe in my world because of this Philosophy. The minute I slip and miss the thought or take on my own will to do things, and then I get into a pickle.

We have so many gifts from God, Our brother Jesus, our Great Spirit, and Spirit helpers. Spirit Communication is the raw material in nature offered to man, by means of which he may if he will, establish communications with those who are in spirit world.

Our manner of using and the purpose, for which this gift is used, is the determining factor to its value to man, both in a positive or negative way. If we choose to abuse our gifts of nature, natural law, or spirit communication, then the value is greatly depreciated. There would be no positive purpose.

When we choose to have a manner of respect and responsibility and a purpose of good for all, then our gifts become very valuable. God or Spirit does not interfere with our choices of use of our natural earth, and natures gifts. Man has choices both positive and negative but………..remember, there is a reaction to mans actions. Nature and Spirit provide for us, we must decide wisely how we use it, and what we do with it.

I get a lot of pleasure out of nature and our beautiful world, which is when I appreciate the value, and handle it with love, respect and responsibility. My wish, my prayer, my belief and hope is that it is that way for all mankind. Take a look around

Spiritual Reflections

you today, and see the world only in a positive way, see your neighbor and fellow brother, as you would see yourself and then act on that with love, respect, and hope.

Thank you to my Spirit Guides that point these things out to me, and thank you God for the gift of spirit. God Bless.

The Green Not of a Spiritualists Life

Good Morning Everyone!

There are so many others that give talks, and we here a lot of great lessons, experiences, and personal changes. It is funny when others share a personal experience and opinion, one can always say "that is just like myself and my life ", or, "Wow that is how it is for me", or, "I hope that never happens to me."

Well my talk may or may not make the wow factor, but it is from personal experiences and opinions I have decided to share.

Where is The Green Eyed Monster?

What's happening to me, why do I find myself trying to become a part of a team and not having an easy time of it? We all hear the term "there is no I in Teamwork" and yet I still witness others trying to put the "I" in.

As everyone knows I am somewhat clairvoyant, and I do sense things that may not be as obvious to others, as it seems to be for me. In my work environment no one truly knows this of me. They do know of my spiritual background, but, not much more than that. Except in my present position in life.

A while back I took a position that would really challenge me in an absolute all inclusive way of my being. I was excited, eager, and very motivated. I had been waiting for this new position. I had completed my University studies, graduated, and going for employment that would challenge me, and ensure use of new lessons.

I was eager, and those who had hired me were also eager. I felt spirit had led me to a path of great challenges, and I discovered they had. I was expected to set up the Psycho Social Medical services for a new agency which would assist people to overcome barriers and personal troubles.

In the beginning with my superior staff all around things went well, everything went well in the growing phase as I like to call it. Everything we do has a growing phase with slips and falls as we get close to any finish line in life.

Six months into the new position though, things began to have changes that were not positive, and at some points seemed to be getting very negative. There was chaos, stressful situations occurred, an increase of insubordination began to happen quite often, staff began to develop clicks, and definitely hated rules, boundaries, and the list of safety rules and checks. Parts of job expectations were being sloughed off. This left the work environment unsafe for some of us.

The more I tried to get everyone to accept the needs of duties as part of the position they were in, the more things became a stress.

I was feeling a very negative energy towards myself. I did however ensure each day I be protected and shielded from this. I kept my positive attitude, and would not compromise my integrity.

Staff began playing with the schedules, scheming to create setups for my failure, and just down right pretending I was not there. Most of the time their schemes back fired, and did not work to their advantage. Although I did have a few uneasy moments.

What bothered me was that this was counter productive to the clients depending on us to help them. The clients would at times comment, "how rude was that," or "wow, do they think they are God or something?" Then there were the clients who would play Houdini and attempt to flee from the place. If I felt the stress I know they sure did as well. This counter productive energy also made it easy for the clients to challenge us with their negative attitudes and behaviors.

Well you get the idea of what it was like. I tried speaking to staff, I tried speaking to my higher ups, and I even prayed harder with my guides to help turn things around. Nothing worked. There were those who said it is jealousy and envy with a little bit of resentment. I thought why would anyone be jealous of me.

When it came time to evaluate how the program was doing and how each of us were doing, it was brought to my attention, staff were trying to set me up for failure, and for failure of the portion of the program I was in. A lot of staff were leaving their positions due to the stress. I was blown away by this.

Here is this program to help people, and here were these green eyed monsters trying to inadvertently destroy the success of the program. Why, it not only harmed myself and the other staff, but it harmed the very ones trusting us to help them and guide them in a positive path. These were troubled clients, and the community trusted us to help them.

I tried to stick it out in the job (as it seemed it was now). It just didn't get better as there was no backing up from the administration part of the program. Then one day, all came to a head, I was looking for a new position, I was surrending to the pressure, I set a time limit for me to exit the job, and asked spirit to help me with this.

Now here is where I say it works, when you leave it in spirits hands. I got home from a very bad day; I then received a phone call, from my old boss. She was just wanting to know How I was doing, and then asked me if I would like to come back and if I could come back to work for her. I of course said if you twist my arm just the right way, sure. She had no Idea what was happening to me in my path. After the call had ended, I sat down and I gave thanks to spirit, as well as meditated on what the next steps were going to be for me, as I transitioned from a negative to a positive.

Well I am happy with my work now, and I feel I have less to worry about in my path, and I definitely know my spirit guides are still with me through thick and thin. I have witnessed and understood spirits astonishing energy to bring about peace and harmony, as well as a healing, as long as I am willing to accept it and do my part.

What I am getting at with this story is that I have to maintain my positive being; I have to give everything I do a good and positive shot towards success for all, the good of mankind. I always work with a positive attitude, and if it is negative, I do my best to change it immediately.

We as spiritualist must continue to build our positive energies, be positive when doing for others or working along side of others. Those who are negative need us to be positive for them, to bring about change. If they are not part of the positive, and don't want to be, that is okay, we just put a sleeve over them and then we do not take on their negative being. I continue to build my being with positive thoughts, beings, and actions. I don't like others tearing down others, just so they can appear better than everyone else; they just want to move the focus of their flaws onto others around them. Picking on others is not acceptable or positive. Talking about others negatively is also not a very good image to me of the one doing it. I see the flaw immediately in those gossipers and their negative being. I also don't believe in criticizing, but in offering a helpful critique to improve the positive way of doing things.

I encourage people to assist, and give help and knowledge were it may be beneficial to others. Instead of negative thinking, try positive thinking. This requires a person to develop a positive personal thought of self, thus changes a negative way of being internally, to a positive. When you see the negative in others it is the mirror image of self you are seeing, change that by building your own thought of abilities and talents in you.

Instead of tearing down of others; try positive thought, being, and acting; try helping the person next to you to succeed. Get rid of Jealousy, by admiring, instead of being, try doing. Envy is not all bad, except if you feel you have to take away negatively in your path. Resentment should be changed to wanting the positive to happen, and then making it happen. If you really want to succeed follow natural law, and personal responsibility, it will amaze you how easy it gets, and how nice it feels to you and your neighbor. May we all find harmony and peace in our path of life? God Bless and thank you.

Law of Love

February reminds us of Ground Hog Day, Presidents Day, Valentines Day, and now Louis Riel Day. I noticed this new Holiday Had a pun to it's meaning by the younger generation as The Real Day that is living the real you. I thought the latter truly rang as the best slogan of the month. Seeing as it fell into place with Heart month and Valentines month. We as humans go sure know how to drum up reasons to send cards, gifts, and celebration invites to others, after all we are social beings.

I have thought about this, and questioned, why is it we need to have a reason to share love and happiness.

Why is it that love, needs a reason to be dolled out in gifts, poetry, and commitment to our loved ones. I never quite get that, I was raised to believe, that love is in all of us, and it should always flow out, for all, with no conditions attached to it. The holidays, are just a fun excuse to get together.

The main thing here is that love be honored when shown and shared. We as Spiritualists honor love each and everyday, and how wonderful that is, and how lucky we are to be Spiritualists. To be able to give love to someone else, one must possess love with in themselves. Actually we don't give love away we share it, as one sows, so shall one receive, is a thought that comes to mind. We have it inside all of us, we just need to let it flow. But in a world of conditions, many people are confused by this conception. How can we just let it flow?

First realize who you are and accept and like yourself for who you are, love yourself. Knowing who you truly are within self, you will then know what you have to offer to others. From this you can also grow, and improve the self, thus having more to share with others. There are all types of love and not restricted to humans. It is essential to all of natures work, natural law, designed and planned very well the entire universe, creating universal love. Unconditional love, pure is as pure as can be possible, as there is no motivation other than being in the love energy and letting it flow to all around.

In a definition of love a dictionary can only give a vague idea of the word love, due to the fact the word has many meanings. Love is passion, affection, sexual attraction, strong or intense liking, natural concern for the welfare of others, the need to embrace, to kiss, and to fuss over… Or a score of zero in tennis. This definition leaves a wide open interpretation for all individuals, and as said confuse some of us.

Dr. Bernie Siegel said," I believe that love banishes all disease and the absence of love is the only true disease." This reference only spoke of the concern for the well being of others in the definition, sometimes called "Brotherly Love". Dr. Peter Breggin stated "Love is what ultimately heals us." In his book "Talking Back to Prozac." Healing results when we have only love in our hearts, and we can only loose the love in our hearts if we allow it to happen. Love it seems is the foundation of truth for healing of illness. Keneth Pelletier of Sanford University backs this up by giving the characteristics of people with optimal health as ones who have a spiritual base, a sense of purpose and belonging, who serve others.

It seems the risk factor for disease to be self centered selfishness. So what's love got to do with it? Everything! One of the laws of nature is, "The Law of God" Love is not just a word, and it is a vibration, a power, an essence. It is Life. The most priceless element in all existence. It cannot be purchased by any means of material life. Love is a dynamic living force, eternal reality, it is spiritual. As love beams out of the human heart, it radiates the love of God. Love is creative, behind every sincere desire and hope, not only eternal it is a very desirable element to possess.

Where or how do we acquire this essence of love?

God gave us this beautiful gift at birth. It is the heritage of every child born on earth. Some of us overflow with abundance of love, for animals, plants, and material means. We are human and our hearts search for affection, sympathy, and love. Love cannot be smothered no matter what. It is the most precious gift of God in its creation, always in demand, and never enough it seems to meet our need.

What can love do for me?

Without love everything would fall apart. Humans cannot function well without love. Love as they say is blind, there are no conditions attached in true love among man. Love does not see scars, blemishes, or ugliness as seen by the human eyes. Love is much deeper and sees beyond the surface. It can heal tenderly the heart of a lonely person. Love sees beyond visible, it is the key to every door, which so many of us seem to misplace.

We spend so much time and energy focusing on worldly possessions. This love of things is unnecessary baggage; you can't take it with you as they say. What is meant by that is the journey to the eternal shores does not require or take in possessions of a materialistic matter. You must find the key to open the door of the temple within. Where love is, where love lives, and where it is latent.

Love is the highest form of vibration that can be attained, love is God, and God is love. Your journey in life is toward the eternal shores, what you do and how you live with self and others, determines the eternal bliss you reach. Why not pave the pathway with love. Jesus in his teachings has taught us how to heal, how to love, and have compassion. Jesus said, "What I can do, you also can do."

The law of love conquers over egotism, not just personal ego, but also in family, race, color, or creed. One helping another with no blockades or stone walls along our paths, love cannot be saved for just certain persons or occasions, it must as any vibration or energy continue to flow freely.

At this time our world needs a lot of healing. We as Spiritualists must come together in sending our love out into the universal energies. Look for the inner beauty in our world, be gracious for the understanding we have, because of the beautiful teachings in Spiritualism.

When the day seems long and hard, you feel people don't care, or you feel the anger, resentment, or negativism of others, look within and find your love of self, rebuild your shield with spirit, ask for help to remove your own negative vibrations, to help fill you with love to send out to those who may be showing it the least, they more than likely need healing. They may not be ready to accept love in healing from anyone, but, send back their vibrations with love.

One never has to accept another's vibration as their own, or allow another's vibrations to affect themselves. There is an expectation amongst people of love and peace, but the reality is one of selfishness and the attacks by the stranger on the weaker or defenseless, does happen. It's so difficult to see these types, because they are good at hiding and disguising their true nature. They are bullies in the truest sense of the word. Bullies are always cowards when they meet their equals or superior peers. This type of person is usually underhanded in actions; they avoid face to face confrontations. They prefer to whisper behind the backs of others, and do not give the victim a chance to represent themselves, no warning, and sadly others respond to this action and inadvertently support the unethical bully. What to do about this?

Remember your spiritual teachings regarding personal responsibility and natural law. No one is excused from their actions just because you were only following another person. Any harm done is your responsibility and you will someday, some how, experience the unflinching result of the natural laws that you miss-used. Refuse to take part in this type of practice send the backstabber, bully, or trouble maker back to the victim, have them confront directly if this is true, you might become the next one on the list of many affected by this behavior.

The choice you make in your actions is very important. To participate or exercise in the act of love and kindness, you cannot have a negative being in action, no matter the reason. Love only happens in the positive vibration, any negativism will nullify the vibration of love, if allowed to flow. Remember if you are the victim forgive, think, feel, and only speak love vibrations. If you think of vengeance and hold a grudge, you keep a negative flow going. You keep the negative vibration inside and cause self to become harmed once again. The one who caused this will not be harmed, and walk away feeling stronger. If you truly desire love and peace, live it. When it is necessary, you may have to stand up for what is right, even if it means risking loosing the battle.

We all want love. But how does it feel? It feels wonderful. Why? Because it connects you to your inner self. Where God truly is, that's one of the reasons that it feels so wonderful. Love strengthens you and those around you, it is positive, bring positive results from the natural laws that are always at work.

Share love freely and you yourself are the big winner and gain the most. If you choose to live without love in your life, you create a life of tension and loneliness. The faces of these people always appear to be sucking lemons. Make note of vengeful, spiteful, and unloving, how they appear in facial looks, even when they try to smile, you will see beyond this, and into their soul. Ask yourself if you would like to be that way. Give love, share love, release spite and hatred, and you'll always benefit more than anyone else.

Love

It is the law

What a gift this talk has been at this point in my life, I questioned my compassion and love of others in my daily life. Due to my own personal experiences in letting my flame of love inside me shrink. It gave way to personal weakness and allowed the bully; or rather the negative person move in and make their move on me. I felt wounded for a while. My Guides however, walked with me and talked with me. I may have forgotten at that moment, but I am now aware of it, and have been guided back to the light of love within me. That flame grows and gives me strength.

I feel I lost the battle with certain people and Experiences, but I have gained back my strength of love and compassion, a major tool for healing. I do not know about the bully's path at this point, but mine is lighter, brighter, and full of love and hope, my faith strengthened. I cannot accept the negative energy, but I can send it back with love.

I can ask daily for my guides to help me remove my negativism, negative energies, beings, and deeds, filling me with the Christ white light, and protecting me with the blue light shield. I can offer myself up as an instrument for spirit to work through for the betterment of man kind, not just for me. Life is not all about me, but, all about the path I journey in, and what I can do now, and what I can leave behind. May every one of God's children know they are loved and blessed with God's energy and light.

Law of Love Part Two

How nice it is to be giving a talk on Mother's Day. A day when we pay respect to our mother's, we honor them for their love and patience they have shown us through the years of growing up. Now to get things straight, we may be children of underprivileged life's, the love we might know, may not be directly from our own mom's for many different reason's, too numerous to run through. I am talking about the nurturing love someone special to us has given us unconditionally. Just like God's love is for us.

    I did a talk not too long ago, on the "Law of Love", I spoke of its power, and how it must not be tied to conditions of any kind to be true and pure, as God had given to each of us. You see God is the universal energy, and a small flame of that loving energy is in each of us, deep within our hearts I believe. When we arrive in this world, we are dependent on the mother we have. We depend on their loving touches, their patient souls, their nurturing manor's, as well as food clothing, and hygiene in our first years. A mother's love is special. As they say, "only A Mother could love that one." Sometimes this is very true. My own experiences as a mother, tell me I was likely not so easy on my Mom at times, and that, thank God I am alive. She could have gone berserk, claimed temporary insanity, and be relieved of me at any given time. I see my mom as a saint at times, oh sure there may have been times she fell from grace, but that is what's so good about unconditional love, it can be forgiven, and all move on with lessons learned. I believe God gave us this reasoning, right about the time we became parents ourselves.

    This could apply to Father's as well, but today it is not Father's Day. You may choose to rehear this talk on that day; it will still be the same, just fill in the required changes as they surface. This is of course part two of the "Law of Love." The best part of the law of love is that it is a part of all the natural laws, it is a natural part of life on earth in the physical manor, and follows us into the spirit life as well. Well getting back on track, there are many types of love in our world, but in this talk I think of a mother's love, Father's love, a child's love, grandparents love, grand child's love, and the animal's love of their human caregivers. There is a theme here; it is love in the living, God's given spark of love.

With this love we can forgive, tolerate, nurture, heal, guide, teach, and many other wonderful things,, like peace, harmony, faith and belief. God gives us this, in the manor of Spirit Guides, Healers, and Protector's. God our creator watches over us, he is forgiving and very patient with all of life's creations. He teaches us through many forms of media, matter, and examples. The lessons are brought through the mouths of others, the mediums ability to receive and deliver messages, the creativity of talent in people through writing, singing, and philosophical discussions. We see messages in what seems like everyday occurrences, but that just suddenly become very apparent when we need an answer the most in our troubled lives.

Guess what, Our Mom's are the biggest answers ever in life. For some reason, they are able to listen with their hearts, not just their ears, amazing isn't it. They let their children rant and rave, cry and pout, kick and scream, become angry and frustrated, then as though none of it took place they say what we need, like it or not. If we are tired, go rest, if we are hungry, go eat, if we are wrong, make it right, if we've been wronged, please forgive. They tear down our cockiness, and build up our confidence. They bring us down to reality, and then we reward by saying, "I hate it when you are always right Mom!", but, we still love you just the same. That part we keep to ourselves. How come moms are so right and so loving?

I believe because God made us that way. From the moment we are born, Mom's forget the pain immediately, because of the beauty and joy that just appeared. The miracle of life, formed from two hearts one soul, and God's spark of light and love. Moms get mad, they are only human, but in being human, they recall the day they received their gift, and forgive what is wronged, and guide and teach what is right. They celebrate with us, our accomplishments, our conquering a weakness and becoming empowered. They guide us through our fears, with philosophical stories of God and heavens activities, such as when thunder occurs and rain begins to fall, that is God's angels that are bowling, and yes even God knocks over a bucket of water every so often when he's washing the floors. Amazing what mom's can do. I hope God keeps making us as good as our mom's ever were, and maybe improve the models as times go on.

I am a mom, and I have watched my daughter become a mom, and she definitely is a top notch model, with extra features and better durability than the last model, but I hear I am being overhauled so that I can be the better grandmother my grandchildren need. All I need do is calm my soul, open my heart, and ask for guidance from my spirit guides, and my higher power. Remembering always give love with no conditions or expectations, and the return of love will be surprisingly special from all around. Love is truly the energy, the elixir, the solvent; of any form of healing we need deep inside us. We all have it; we just need to nurture our inner love, with love, that God gave us. What we are looking for from elsewhere really is just inside our own hearts waiting to be released. If we give ourselves what we expect from others or other things, we will not need to look for it elsewhere, but we will be able to give it away, unconditionally. I see children as the best example, and the even better example is within the special needs children and adult children. They are very durable, easily hurt, but get over it quickly, and move on with forgiveness and love no matter who you are. God gave us these special hearted people to remind us, love is not complicated, it knows no way to hurt or destroy. It only seeks to nurture, heal, and grow within all; love is after all a natural law. Don't fight it embrace it, and if nothing else hug a mother, your mother, or anybody else's mother. I figure I have at least eight adopted mothers in my life. They are not hard to find, because they are within all of us, yes guys included.

I thank God for Mother's, Dad's, and Children they are in his guiding hands, and spirits challenges to guide and protect. God Bless, and happy Mother's day.

God's Loving Laws to Live By

These past few weeks I have encountered people who are feeling lost and confused, scared and angry at themselves, and finding it hard to live with themselves. They find themselves depressed, and barely getting through the day without falling apart. One recent encounter brought me back in time remembering my own difficulties, with the evils of addiction, and compulsive behaviors.

In listening to others share, I was reminded how bad things were at one point for me, but that now my life is good, it has direction, it has meaning. I have developed compassion and empathy for others around me, those that suffer from their shortcomings, and character defects.

It reminds me of my struggles to give up the negatives in my life, watching them struggle to do the same.

It is amazing to me, that at one time, I thought I will never survive the changes that I must make, to develop into a person who is a part of societies normal expectations in the community. Now I find myself reassuring the struggling person, that they too will make it, if they honestly want to. The key is the honesty to self. I guide the individual to look within self to find the love, compassion, forgiveness to self. Start there and work from those key elements to change and improve they life and path they are on. I assure them there is only one day they need to start with, and that is today. I talk to them; I listen as hard as I can to them. I confirm what they are saying to me so they can hear themselves, and what they are saying about themselves. I try to get those in need to try and talk about themselves, and say it back like it were a third party person we were speaking about.

In doing this I can ask as well "if it were someone else you were talking about, that you cared about, what would you want to say to them? How would you want to treat them, with compassion, and love?" I would want them to love this person within them, and work toward supporting them.

I did not learn this from a book, or psychologist. I learned this technique from a twelve step program, and my journey to building my spirit self back up. I had to learn about, and understand, that there is a simple but good way to live, that is to live with God's love in my heart, and God's natural laws to give me guidance and direction in living and making my life path a positive journey. I share these natural laws with those I want to help, and so that I don't forget them myself, I live by them by day, and I sleep well at night because I do this, for myself and those I come in contact with each day in my path. With God's love, and help, and the help of those spirit guides he provides, my life is beautiful.

Okay, so recently my daughter was deathly ill, but, she pulled through, with the help of guides, and the well learned doctor's of medicine, she is okay, and out living her life. I got through another scare in life. This is all because I trust and believe in the power of healing and natural law.

There are really only a small number of natural laws to learn about and live within, that are not so hard to do, once you begin to practice them in your daily life, it is like breathing air, you need it to survive, and to live well.

"Natural Law" is that law God put in motion, which governs all that he has created. You cannot try to change it or ignore it, unless of course you want to struggle going against natural law. So many times man has tried to manipulate this set of natural laws, only to have disaster come to them, and those that may be around them.

"The Law of Life" that of which develops the relationship between God, and Man. It is the ability to adjust our self to it and strengthen the power of God that is expressed through us.

"The Law of Love" is a creative force for all life, it is the highest vibration that can be attained, love is God, and God is love. If you love, you will be loved. God is within each of us, like a spark of light energy, if we allow it to radiate outward, it will strengthen and be returned to each of us.

"The Law of Truth" speaks for itself really. It is right thinking, right acting, and right living. Honesty within oneself is the ability to live honestly among your fellow man. Truth always prevails they say, and it does. It is far easier to start living honestly, and dumping the dishonesty. Dishonesty creates a funnel like a tornado, you have to be on top of it, or it will go uncontrollably wrong, with a disastrous affect to self and others. Truth is of good vibrations, dishonesty is of unsettling vibrations. We must always strive to live a life of the highest and best vibration afforded to each of us. We have that choice.

"The Law of Compensation" Just payment for ones own personal acts in his daily path in life. If you are bad, then payment is bad as well, if you are good, good will be your payment. The law of compensation exacts its punishment or reward. Do acts of kindness and kindness will be returned? Start off small and humble, sincere in what you are able to do, time will strengthen, and will increase your ability to be kind in many different manners.

"The Law of Freedom" We have unlimited power of choice, we can live as we desire, and we will either suffer for the bad choices, or progress in accordance of those desires that do good for the betterment of all.

The best way to remember any natural law is to remember, "Whatsoever ye would that others should do unto you, do ye also unto them". Provide a positive surround to self and those around, and naturally you will feel that same from those around you.

Keep on the positive even if feeling the negative and it soon turns around for you.

Don't force something to go a certain way, let it flow, then nothing gets broken, or lost. Keep it simple, be who it is you want to be, as long as you are comfortable in that role, and can live within yourself as that person you want to be. Remember too, it is never too late to start to live a positive life, and as each day rolls by, it will get easier and increasingly more positive in your life path. Mold yourself to who you want to be and love. Love from within, rely on who you are, and be authentic and original. We can all act like someone else, but then we never know our real self being. Tell yourself each morning I love myself enough to do right by myself, and at night, tell yourself how much you love being you, and give thanks to the loving God we have and his natural laws he gave us to love and live by.

God Bless, and once again Thank you Dr. Silvers, and Firebird for inspiring me.

About This Book;

I wrote this book over a time of many years, that is the writings were done over several years, I have written more than the ones contained in this book, but, I chose these writings as they were received very well by those who listened to them when I delivered them as talks (sermons to some) in church services. The writings are based on life's experiences and the meditations I do each day. My connection with Spirit World, allows me to hear the messages Spirit gives me. I started writing these messages down as I received them, until I was able to compile short writings to give as talks to the members of the church I attend. I hope it is enjoyed by you the reader.

About The Author:

I was born on the west coast, but my family moved to the prairies when I was young, so I grew up there. I attended public school for the most part, Worked at a young age, graduated High School, and married soon after to my first real boyfriend. I knew very little about life, and had a lot of struggles, and sad moments in my life. Writing I feel gave me an outlet, and saved me at times. I have three grown children and four grandchildren, and I am very proud of all of them. I grew up with my children and still am growing up, that is I still have more to journey in my life path. I have discovered a lot about me in my journey, and I think the writings I have done tell of the journey and the wisdom I gain from looking at my life and recognizing what I am learning. My walk with Spirit, and my talking with Spirit have made these writings possible, I do hope you enjoy them. God Bless

    White Fawn (Doris)

Notes

Notes

Notes

Notes

Notes

Notes

Notes

Notes

Notes

Notes

Notes

Notes

Notes

Notes

Notes

Notes

Notes

Notes